Th Food Recipes From North India

A Cookbook of 23 Popular Northern Indian Dishes

By Meera Joshi

More books by Meera Joshi:

Disclaimer

All reasonable efforts have been made to provide accurate and error-free recipes within this book. These recipes are intended for use by persons possessing the appropriate technical skill, at their own discretion and risk. It is advisable that you take full note of the ingredients before mixing and use substitutes where necessary, to fit your dietary requirements.

Contents

Introduction

This cookbook showcases the fantastic flavors of the states and union territories of Northern India. Here, I celebrate the true uniqueness that Northern culture has brought to Indian cuisine; whether a popular dish such as curry, which in the North comprises of thick, spicy and creamy gravies or whether a popular Northern ingredient such as dry fruits, regularly used as a main ingredient in the region.

Northern India is well represented by the cuisines of eight states; Jammu & Kashmir, Uttar Pradesh, Haryana, Rajasthan, Himachal Pradesh, Uttarakhand and two union territories; Delhi and Chandigarh. It is rich in culture due to the North being the historical centre of the Mughals, Delhi Sultanate and British Indian Empires. Mughal cuisine is one of the most famous cuisines throughout Northern India, thanks to its distinct spices, responsible for producing wonderful flavors. Similarly, Punjabi cuisine is famous for its spiciness, distinctive aroma, taste and unique style of cooking. Within the state of Utter Pradesh, the city of Lucknow has produced world famous cuisine, known as 'Awadhi', possessing a strong Central Asian influence.

Many Indian restaurants around the globe have been influenced by Northern Indian cuisine over the years. Chefs who had migrated from Punjab, blended food from the North with cuisine from around the world to create a fusion that is truly unique and special. The Nawabs of Awadh (Lucknow) were great gourmets and encouraged their master chefs to create a new style of cooking that is now famous in all Indian restaurants, homes and throughout the whole world.

In the North it is preferred to use lamb and goat in many dishes, if you are a fan of these meats then you'll discover recipes that enhance these taste sensations.

However Northern Indian cuisine compliments any type of meat or dietary requirement, I have also included fantastic fish, chicken and vegetarian dishes all of which are favorites within the Northern states.

This is 23 of the best recipes from the North of India, welcome to a region of world-famous unique cuisine. Enjoy!

FREE Bonuses

We have 3 **FREE** bonus recipe ebooks for your enjoyment!

- **Cookie Cookbook** 2134 recipes
- **Cake Cookbook** 2444 recipes
- **Mac and Cheese Cookbook** 103 recipes

Simply visit: www.ffdrecipes.com to get your **FREE** recipe ebooks.

You will also receive free exclusive access to our VIP World Recipes Club, giving you FREE best-selling book offers, discounts and recipe ideas, delivered to your inbox regularly.

Mountain Meat Curry

This spicy curry is a famous dish from the state of Uttarakhand and is a perfect curry to provide some warmth on a cold day. The garlic sauce is very popular in the region.

Serves – 5 persons
Time – 60 minutes

Ingredients

For the Sauce
1 tsp chopped garlic
1 tsp cumin seeds
1 tsp coriander seeds
½ tsp turmeric powder
Red chilli powder to taste
Salt to taste

For main preparation
½ kg meat (cut into shapes)
3 tbsp chopped onions
2 tbsp oil
3 tbsp prepared sauce
2 tbsp chopped tomato
1 ½ cup of water

Preparation

1.   Grind together all the spices; garlic, cumin seeds, coriander seeds, salt, red chilli powder and turmeric powder, forming a paste.
2.   Heat oil in a pan, add chopped onions and fry until translucent.
3.   Now add the prepared sauce and mix them well.

4. To the mixture add chopped tomatoes and stir until well cooked.

5. Now add the meat followed by water and mix. Cover the pan and seal with wheat balls. Leave to cook for half an hour over low heat.

6. Serve hot.

Best served with - rice or chapattis.

Chicken Tikka Masala

Originating from the Northern state of Punjab, this dish has become one of the most popular Indian dishes internationally. The recipe makes good use of the masalas, chili blend and creamy sauce. The meat is marinated first on skewers, cooked, then cooked once more in its own sauce.

Serves - 4 persons
Time -60 minutes

Ingredients

Chicken tikkas:

Bamboo or metal skewers

¾ cup plain, full-fat yogurt

3-4-inch ginger, peeled and cut into chunks

3 cloves of garlic cut into chunks

4 tbsp fresh chopped cilantro

2 tsp coriander powder

1 tsp cumin powder

2 tsp ground Kashmiri chilies

1 ½ tsp kosher salt

½ tsp Punjabi garam masala

½ tsp turmeric, ground

1 ½ lb boneless, skinless chicken breasts cut into medium cubes

For the sauce:

2 tbsp ghee, butter or oil of your choice

1 small yellow or red onion, coarsely chopped

1 small red bell pepper, stemmed, seeded and cubed

¼ cup slivered blanched almonds

¼ cup golden raisins

2 medium tomatoes, diced

¼ cup heavy cream or half-and-half

4 tbsp plain, full-fat yogurt

½ tsp coarse kosher salt

¼ tsp cayenne

¼ tsp Punjabi garam masala

Cilantro, chopped

Preparation

1. Prepare the chicken tikka marinade by first making a paste out of the garlic, ginger, cilantro and chilies by either mashing them using a pestle and mortar with some salt into a paste or using a food processor. In a medium sized bowl, combine the yogurt, ginger and garlic paste, coriander, cumin, salt, garam masala, and turmeric into a small bowl. Whisk to blend.

2. Add the chicken cubes to the sauce and using your hands, toss to combine and ensure that the sauce covers the chicken. Next, cover the chicken and refrigerate for 2 hours or overnight, recommended in order to marinate.

4. Next day, when ready to cook, prepare the sauce by heating the ghee, oil or butter in a medium sized saucepan. Add the onions, bell peppers, almonds and raisins to the pan, cook stirring frequently until the onions are caramelized, 12-15 minutes.

5. If using a grill, ensure it is prepared and ready to go. Alternately you can cook the chicken in the oven at 425 F. Ensue the oven is pre-heated first.

6. Stir the tomatoes into the pan and stir to deglaze any caramelized vegetables. Cook for 2 to 5 minutes.

7. Remove from the heat. Add the cream, yogurt, salt, cayenne and garam masala. Stir to combine. Let the mixture cool. Puree in a food processor. Return the sauce back to its sauce pan.

8. Grill the chicken or if using oven, line the chicken skewers and place in the oven. Check every 8-10 minutes for doneness and to turn the skewers to ensure all sides are cooked well.

Best served with – any variation of flatbreads or with steamed Basmati rice.

Radish Root with Potato Curry

A local vegetarian dish from the mountains of Uttarakhand, containing mountain radish roots with potatoes. In this dish, the radish is not cut into pieces but crushed (known as thinchao).

Serves – 4 persons
Time – 40 minutes

Ingredients

4 radish roots
1 potato
2 tbsp oil or clarified butter
A pinch of asafoetida
5 cloves of garlic
3 cm piece of ginger
1 medium chopped onion
1 medium chopped tomato
1 tsp cumin seeds or dry faran leaves
5 red chillies
½ tsp red chilli powder
½ tsp coriander powder
½ tsp turmeric powder
6 cups of water
Salt to taste

Preparation

1. Wash, peel and crush the radish and potato. Then peel and crush the ginger and garlic cloves.

2. Place oil in a frying pan over medium heat. Next add crushed garlic and ginger and stir fry. Then add crushed radish and potato and fry the mixture for a further 3-4 minutes. Set aside.

3. With the remaining oil add cumin seeds, red chillies, asafoetida, and chopped onion, fry until light brown in color. Now add the red chilli powder, turmeric powder, coriander powder and fry for 4-5 seconds.

4. Add all the fried vegetables kept aside followed by chopped tomatoes, salt and some water. Boil for 3 minutes.

5. Now add remaining water and pressure cook or cook for 30 minutes over low heat until the radish becomes tender. Spread over coriander leaves and green chillies (split into two halves). Serve it hot.

Best served with - steamed rice or puffed chapattis.

Pashtun Chicken Fry

This dish is from the state of Punjab but also very popular in Pakistan. It is regularly sold by street side vendors making it easily available whilst travelling through Punjab.

Serves – 4 persons
Time – 30 minutes

Ingredients

1/4 tea spoon turmeric powder
¼ tea spoon citric acid
2 star anise
1 piece of ginger
1 kg whole chicken
Salt to taste
½ bunch finely chopped mint leaves
Oil to fry
10 cloves of crushed garlic
4 cinnamon stick (1 inch sized)
¼ tea spoon turmeric powder
6 green cardamom
½ mace
½ tea spoon royal cumin seeds
½ tea spoon cumin seeds
¼ tea spoon mustard seeds
4 whole dry red chillies

Preparation

1. Firstly, cut the chicken into two halves and apply gashes over it.

2. Now within a bowl add ginger, garlic pieces, whole spices (star anise, cinnamon stick, green cardamom, mace, black cumin seeds) cumin seeds, mustard seeds, red chillies, turmeric powder, salt, mint leaves and add all to a blender and make a paste of it.

3. Now apply the spice paste all over the chicken and let it marinate for 1 hour 45mins. Then place the chicken pieces into a steamer and steam for 10 minutes. Leave to cool so the spice paste remains stuck to the chicken.

4. Now place a sufficient amount of oil into a pan and deep fry the chicken pieces on both sides. Serve hot.

Best served with - chips and salad (as a snack).

Lamb Feet Curry

An authentic curry prepared with lamb feet in thick gravy. Famous in the state of Uttar Pradesh and especially in Awadh (Lucknow).

Serves – 4 persons
Time – 85 minutes

Ingredients

1 tsp turmeric powder
1 tbsp ginger garlic paste
1 sprig curry leaves
1 chopped onion
3 bay leaves
2 cardamom
2 cinnamon
1 tsp royal cumin seeds
2 cloves
2 tbsp oil
8 lamb legs
Salt to taste
3 whole green chillies
1 tbsp freshly made coconut powder
1 tbsp coriander powder
½ tsp ground spices powder
½ tsp pepper powder
1 tsp red chilli powder
1 bunch coriander leaves
Water as required

Preparation

1. Take the lamb legs apply a little turmeric and water, clean them and set aside.

2. Now take a pressure cooker and add oil followed by cardamom, cloves, cinnamon, caraway seeds, bay leaves and chopped onions, then mix them for a while. Add the curry leaves, ginger-garlic paste, turmeric powder, green chillies and salt to taste, while mixing well once again.

3. Next add lamb legs to the spice mixture, mix and add water as required. Place lid on pressure cooker and leave to cook for 35 minutes over low heat.

4. Once the lamb legs are well cooked add coconut powder, coriander powder, ground spices powder, pepper powder, red chilli powder and mix.

5. Cook for another 15 minutes and if more soup is required add water as required.

6. Finally, add chopped coriander leaves. Serve hot.

Best served with - any kind of Chapattis.

Dry Beans Berry Recipe

This is a traditional Rajasthani dish, made with various spices and highly popular in the region as a regular dish.

Serves – 6 persons
Time – 60 minutes

Ingredients

Coriander leaves
75 grams berries
75 grams dried beans
2 tsp oil
2 tsp ginger-garlic paste
6 whole red chillies
1 tsp mango powder
1 tsp coriander powder
1 tsp red chilli powder
1 tsp turmeric powder
1 tsp cumin seeds
6 pieces of dried mango
1 tsp salt
Fried garlic
3½ tsp yogurt
Whole fried red chillies

Preparation

1. Soak the berries and dried beans in beaten yogurt. Keep overnight.
2. Boil for 20 minutes and clean them with water.

3. Heat oil in a pan, add dried mango pieces, ginger-garlic paste, cumin seeds, coriander powder, turmeric powder, whole red chillies, red chilli powder, mango pieces and curd. Sauté the spices well.

4. Now add berries and dried beans with salt, mix well. Leave to cook for a while. For the final touch, apply fried garlic, coriander leaves, fried whole red chillies. Serve hot.

Best served with - chapattis.

Dal Makhani

Dal Makhani is an extremely popular dish, originating from the Punjab region. The dish mainly consists of all black gram with red beans, butter and cream.

Serves: 2 persons
Time: 40 minutes

Ingredients

1/4 cup whole black gram
1 tbsp red kidney beans
1/2 tsp red chilli powder
Ginger chopped 1 inch pieces
1-1/2 tbsp non-dairy butter
1/2 tbsp oil
1/2 tsp cumin seeds
3 cloves garlic chopped

1/2 onion chopped

1 green chilies slit

1 tomatoes

1/2 tsp garam masala powder

Salt to taste

Preparation

1. Wash whole black gram and red kidney beans and soak in three cups of water.

2. Boil whole black gram and red kidney beans in three cups of water with salt and half of red pepper powder for three whistles in pressure cooker. Open the lid and see if the Red kidney beans is completely smooth. Otherwise simmer until the Red kidney beans are completely smooth.

3. In a pan over medium heat, add oil, butter and cumin seeds. Once seeds change color, sauté with onion, garlic and ginger.

4. Add Chopped green chilies, tomatoes and saute over high heat. Add the rest of the red chili powder and cook until the tomatoes are reduced to a paste.

5. Add the cooked Red kidney beans and black gram with the cooking liquid. Add a little water if the mixture is too thick. Add the garam masala powder and adjust salt.

6. Simmer until dals are completely smooth.

7. Serve hot.

Best served with – Rice

Rogan Josh

Rogan Josh is considered to be a traditional dish of the Kashmiri or North Western part of India. It showcases the region's ingredients such as Kashmiri chilies.

Serves - 6 persons
Time – 60 minutes

Ingredients

¼ cup Greek yogurt or plain yogurt strained overnight
6-8 garlic cloves, peeled and crushed into a paste like consistency
2-3 inch ginger, peeled and smashed into paste like consistency in mortar pestle or food processor
2 tsp Bin bhuna hua garam masala or garam masala of your choice
2 tsp salt, or to taste
1 ½ lb of boneless leg of lamb, fat trimmed and discarded, cut into 1-inch cubes

For Frying

2-3tbsp butter, ghee or oil of your choice

1 tsp cumin seeds

1 tsp fennel seeds

10-12 whole cloves

4 black or green cardamom pods

8-10 curry leaves or 2 fresh or dried bay leaves

2 cinnamon sticks

1 medium onion, finely chopped

1 medium tomato, cubed

1tbsp Kashmiri chilies or a combination of ¼ tbsp cayenne mixed with ½ tbsp sweet paprika

Preparation

1) Whisk the yogurt together with ginger and garlic paste along with garam masala and salt together in a medium-sized bowl. Add the lamb and stir to coat with the marinade. Cover and refrigerate for several hours or overnight.

2) On the day of cooking, heat ghee, butter or oil over a wide-skillet over medium heat. Sprinkle with cumin seeds, fennel seeds, cloves, cardamom pods, bay leaves or curry leaves and cinnamon sticks. Stir and cook until spices emit a fragrance. Approximately 30 secs to a minute.

3) Add the onions and cook until caramelized or golden brown 6-8 minutes. Add the tomatoes and cook for a few minutes longer.

4) Over medium heat, add the lamb marinade along with its sauce and cook, stirring occasionally until yogurt is absorbed by the lamb and the ghee is starting to separate from the meat, about 15-10 minutes.

5) Stir in the chilies and stir the mixture to make sure the lamb pieces get coated with the paste. Pour 1 cup of water and stir once or twice to deglaze the skillet. Bring the mixture to boil. Reduce the heat, cover the pan and simmer, stirring occasionally to prevent the curry from sticking to the bottom.
6) Cook until the lamb is cooked through and tender, approximately 20-25 minutes.

Best served with – Naan or with steamed Basmati rice

Charcoal Grilled Chicken

Prepared regularly in Punjab, this is a popular form of street food. A charcoal grill is used to cook the chicken with lots of added spices.

Serves – 4 persons
Time – 50 minutes

Ingredients
7-8 chicken legs
Clarified butter (for basting)

For Marination
3 tbsp cooking oil
4 ½ tsp strained garlic paste
3 ½ strained ginger paste
3 tbsp whisked yogurt
4 tbsp malt vinegar
2 tsp freshly roasted and coarsely grounded black pepper
1 ½ tsp cinnamon powder
dried fenugreek leaf powder (a pinch)
1 ½ tsp black cardamom powder
1 ½ tsp cumin powder
1 tsp green cardamom powder
1 tsp clove powder
1 tsp all spices powder
½ tsp mace powder
¼ tsp nutmeg powder
1 ½ tsp coriander powder
1 tsp nutmeg powder
2 tsp pomegranate powder
salt to taste

Preparation

1. Take the chicken legs and clean them and make deep angular incisions, 3 on each thigh and 2 on the drumsticks.
2. In a wok, heat oil, add ginger then garlic and stir fry until moisture evaporates. Remove from heat and stir with yogurt, mix well. Place mixture in a bowl to cool.
3. To prepare the marinade, mix the remaining ingredients. Rub marinade into the chicken legs. Set aside for 6 hours in a bowl.
4. Roast marinated chicken legs over a charcoal grill, over medium heat for 7 minutes, turning each chicken leg and basting with clarified butter.
5. Remove chicken legs from grill and separate thigh bone from drumstick bone, carefully leaving meat intact. Once again place them on the grill and cook for another 3-4 minutes, turning them and basting once. Serve hot with Mint-coriander sauce (chutney).

Best served - as a snack and side dish for lunch or dinner.

Trout Recipe

A famous dish from the region of Himachal Pradesh. In this dish the fish is smeared with a host of Indian spices and served with hot rice.

Serves – 4 persons
Time – 85 minutes

Ingredients
1 trout

For marinade
½ tsp salt
1 tsp dill leaves
1 tsp coriander seeds (crushed)
¼ tsp red chilli flakes
½ tsp lemon rind
2 tsp lemon juice
1 tbsp mustard oil

For the sauce
2 tbsp mustard oil
½ tsp mustard seeds
1 ½ tbsp diced onions
1 tsp chopped coriander
2 tsp lemon juice
¼ tsp salt

Preparation

1. Clean and wash the trout nicely. Take a bowl and add the fish, salt, dill leaves, crushed coriander seeds, chilli flakes, lemon rind, lemon juice and mustard oil.
2. Apply the marinade mixture all over the fish and keep it aside for 10 minutes.
3. Add oil to a pan and heat, then add the pieces of marinated fish and fry them on both sides under a low heat for 10 minutes.
4. Again, add oil to a pan and heat. Add mustard seeds and onions and sauté until brown in color. Remove from heat and add lemon juice, coriander leaves, and salt. Mix well.
5. Pour on sauce. Serve hot.

Best served with - steamed rice.

Stuffed Sole Fish

This dish is very popular in the state of Uttar Pradesh. The preparation is rustic in nature as the stuffed fish is prepared in a sealed earthenware case.

Serves – 4 persons
Time – 60 minutes

Ingredients
1 kg sole fish
250 gm curd
100 gm gram flours
150 gm flour (for sealing)
50 gm aniseed powder
25 gm caraway powder
25 gm desiccated coconut
15 gm almonds peeled
15 gm pistachio nuts
20 gm cuddapah almond
20 gm poppy seeds (lightly roasted)
20 gm ginger
20 gm garlic
1 tsp chilli powder
Mace 2 blades
6 cloves
6 pepper corns
4 black cardamom
A pinch of edible orange color
1 tsp lemon juice
1 tsp oil
Salt to taste

Preparation

1. Firstly, skin the fish, wash and slit one side. Apply salt and squeeze a lemon over. Set aside for 20 minutes. Meanwhile prepare a paste of ginger and garlic.
2. Next make a paste from the peeled almonds, lightly roasted poppy seeds, cuddapah almond and desiccated coconut. Blanch and peel the pistachio nuts and chop finely. Then make a grinded paste of mace, cardamom, cloves and peppercorns.
3. Dissolve the edible color in 1 tsp of water and spread it over the marinated fish. Mix all the ingredients in a bowl aside from the pistachio nuts. Stuff the fish with the mixture and pistachio nuts.
4. Take a flat earthenware and grease it with oil. Place the fish over it and seal the mouth of the earthenware then bury it below the ground. Now place charcoal over the earthenware and light fire from above. Cook for 6 hours over low flame. This can also be done in a microwave within an hour.
5. Finally take out the seal and serve hot.

Best served with - Handkerchief bread (Roomali roti).

Gatte Ki Sabzi

Gatte ki Sabzi is an essential dish, if you enjoy Rajasthani food. Typically made with besan (Gram) flour, these are delicious dumplings in a great tasting sauce.

Serves – 2 persons
Time - 50 minutes

Ingredients

1 cup gram flour
3/4 cup non-dairy yogurt (whisked)
1/2 inch ginger (chopped)
1/8 tsp soda bicarbonate
1/4 cup mawa (khoya)
1/4 cup paneer (cottage cheese)
1 green chilies chopped
1 tbsp oil
1/2 tsp cumin seeds
1 /2 tbsp red chilli powder
1 tbsp coriander powder
1/8 tsp asafoetida
1/2 tsp turmeric powder
1 /2 cup tomato paste
1/4 tsp garam masala powder
Salt to taste

Preparation

1. Mix flour with ginger, salt, baking soda. Continue to add water in order to make a stiff dough. Knead and set aside.
2. Grate mawa and paneer. Add green chilies and salt. Mix well.

3. Separate flour dough into small ball sized portions. Using mawa-paneer mixture, stuff into each ball. Achieve a cylindrical shape.
4. Add three cups of salted water to a pan, add the stuffed gate and boil for 15 minutes. Leave to drain.
5. Preparation for the sauce; heat the oil, add the cumin seeds, brown then add red chili powder, coriander, turmeric powder and asafoetida. Cook until the oil begins to separate. Add the tomato paste.
6. Reduce heat and add the remaining yogurt, stirring constantly. Add Garam masala powder and salt. Add gatte and cook until sauce thickens.
7. Serve hot.

Best served with – rice and chapattis

Royal Dessert

This is a rich dessert recipe from Kashmir. Living up to its name, it contains the very best of flavors!

Serves – 4 persons
Time – 30 minutes

Ingredients

8 slices of white bread
2 cup milk
4 tbsp of sugar
½ tsp cardamom powder
Clarified butter for frying
Pistachio nuts

Preparation

1.   Slice bread into round shapes.
2.   In a pan, add clarified butter and fry bread slices. Set aside.
3.   Boil the milk slowly and reduce it to quarter, while continuously stirring to make condensed milk.
4.   Next add cardamom powder and spread the condensed milk (rabdi) over the fried bread pieces, and embellish with chopped pistachio nuts.

Best served - after lunch or dinner.

Butter Chicken

This creamy chicken dish is popular among the mainstream Indian restaurants around the world. It hails from the northern part of India where cream and tomato are commonly used in dishes to achieve a tangy and creamy balance.

Serves - 4-6 persons
Time – 60 minutes

Ingredients

1 ½ cups full-fat Greek yogurt
2 tbsp lemon juice
2 tbsp ground turmeric
1 tsp coriander powder
½ tsp ground black pepper
1 tsp cayenne
½ tsp ground cardamom
2 tbsp ground cumin
3 lbs chicken thighs, bone-in

1 stick unsalted butter

5 tsp oil (neutral in flavor like canola)

2 medium-sized yellow onions, peeled and diced

4 cloves garlic, peeled and minced

3 tbsp fresh ginger, peeled and grated or finely diced

1 tbsp cumin seeds

1 cinnamon stick

3 medium-sized tomatoes, diced

2 spicy chilies such as serrano or jalapeno or Anaheim, diced

1 ½ tsp, salt to taste

1 ½ cups cream

2/3 cups water

3 tbsp almond meal or almonds finely chopped

8 oz fresh or frozen peas

Handful of fresh cilantro, chopped with stems removed

Preparation:

1) In a medium-sized bowl, create a sauce by adding yogurt, lemon juice, turmeric, coriander, black pepper, cayenne, cardamom and cumin. Add chicken and with your hands coat to cover the chicken thighs. Refrigerate the chicken in a container with a cover overnight or for at least 4 hours.

2) On the day of cooking, heat a large pan over medium high heat. Add the oil and let it heat for a few minutes. Add butter and cook until it starts to foam. Add the onions, stirring frequently. Cook until translucent and slightly caramelized. Add garlic, ginger and cumin seeds and cook until the onions start to become golden brown.

3) Add the cinnamon stick, tomatoes, chilies and salt to the mixture and continue to cook stirring frequently. Add peas and water and bring the mixture to a boil, then lower the heat and simmer uncovered for 25 to 30 minutes.
4) Stir in the cream and simmer for an additional 10 to 15 minutes., until the chicken is cooked through.
5) Add the almond meal or chopped almonds and cook for 5 minutes longer. Remove from the heat and garnish with fresh chopped cilantro.

Best served with –steamed Basmati rice, also wonderful on its own.

Mutton Liver Recipe

One of the most popular recipes in Uttar Pradesh is the Mutton liver recipe, it is very common in almost every corner of the state, especially in Lucknow (Awadh).

Serves – 4 persons
Time – 50 minutes

Ingredients

½ kg liver washed and wiped dry
½ tsp ginger paste
½ tsp garlic paste
½ tsp chilli powder
¼ cup of yogurt
¼ tsp grounded spices
Salt to taste
2 tbsp clarified butter
½ cup of grated onions
2 tbsp coriander leaves
Lemon wedges

Preparation

1. Chop liver into small pieces.
2. In a large bowl add ginger-garlic paste, chilli powder, yogurt, grounded spices, salt and the liver. Mix well.
3. In a pan, add clarified butter and heat. Next add onions and sauté until golden brown.
4. Then add the liver mixture to the pan and sauté until the fat separates.
5. Now add ½ cup of water and pressure cook for 5 minutes.

6. Continue to stir fry until the water completely dries out and the fat becomes separated.
7. The dish is ready to be served embellished with coriander leaves and lemon wedges.

Best served - at dinner or lunch and combines well with Pulao or Biriyani.

Moringa Flowers Recipe

This is a very popular and healthy Sindhi recipe using drumstick flowers, originating from the state of Punjab.

Serves – 4 persons
Time – 30 minutes

Ingredients

¼ tsp red chilli powder
250 gm drumstick flowers
1 tbsp beaten curd
¼ tsp turmeric powder
¼ cup of tomato puree
1 finely chopped green chilli
1 tsp ginger-garlic paste
½ tsp coriander powder
1 pinch grounded spices
1 finely chopped onion

Preparation

1. Firstly, clean the drumstick flowers and remove any stem parts from the buds /bloomed flowers. Boil them in water for 5-6 minutes. Cool and squeeze off the water, then repeat the boiling process 3-4 times.
2. Add the oil in a pan, heat it and add onions. Fry until golden brown.
3. Next add the green chillies and roast then add ginger-garlic paste.
4. Add the prepared flowers and sauté until it becomes dried.
5. Now add spices and tomato puree. Cook until the recipe becomes dry.

6. Add the curd and cook the preparation for another 4 minutes.

7. Mash well with a masher and add a pinch of grounded spice. Serve hot.

Best served with - any kind of chapattis.

Saag Paneer (Indian Cheese in Fragrant Spinach Sauce)

For natives living in the north of India, Indian cheese is a delicacy saved for special occasions. The state of Punjab is the birth place of this great dish. An onion-cumin-fenugreek-laced spinach sauce is used to cook this recipe.

Serves - 4 persons
Time – 40 minutes

Ingredients:

8-oz Paneer Indian Cheese, cubed

1 lb fresh spinach or 8 oz frozen spinach

1 tbsp dried fengugreek leaves

5 tbsp ghee or oil

2 tsp cumin

1 medium onion, chopped

2-inch knob of fresh ginger, grated or diced finely

1 tsp turmeric

2 hot green chilies such as serrano or jalapeno, minced

1 tsp salt or to taste

2 tsp garam masala

Preparation

1. Saute the paneer in a skillet by heating 2 tbsp of oil or ghee over medium-high heat. Add the paneer cubes and sauté until golden brown in color and set aside.

2. Cook the spinach by blanching it in hot boiling water for 2-3 minutes. Drain and set aside.

3. Make the sauce by heating 4 tbsp of oil in a large pan over medium-high heat. Add the cumin seeds and wait for it to sizzle. Add the onions and ginger. Cook by stirring frequently for 2 minutes. Add the turmeric, chilies and stir to cook for a few seconds.

4. Add the Spinach and fenugreek puree to the sauce along with 1 cup water, add salt. Raise the heat and bring the mixture to boil. Lower the heat and continue to simmer.

5. Add the paneer slices and garam masala. Continue to simmer for a few more minutes. Taste, then adjust the salt to taste.

6. Serve hot.

Best served with - any variation of flatbreads or with steamed Basmati rice.

Colocasia Roots Curry

A popular dish in the mountains of Himachal Pradesh. It is a great tasting curry in which colocasia roots are prepared in yogurt gravy.

Serves – 4 persons
Time – 40 minutes

Ingredients

500 gm boiled Colocasia roots
Mustard oil
Salt to taste
½ tsp red chilli powder
1 tsp coriander powder
1 cup sour buttermilk
2 green chillies
4 garlic pods
1 Strand onion greens
5 tbsp rice flour
½ tsp turmeric powder

Preparation

1. Make a coarse paste of the red chillies, onion greens, garlic pods and onion white. Set aside.
2. Now coat the Colocasia roots with 2 tbsp rice flour and shallow fry with mustard oil.
3. Take a pan, add mustard oil and heat. Add the coarse paste prepared earlier and stir for a while.
4. In a bowl, mix 3 tbsp rice flour with sour buttermilk, mix well. Place in a pan and stir once more.

5. Next add fried Colocasia roots, red chilli powder, coriander powder, turmeric powder and salt. Cook 5-6 minutes and serve hot.

Best served with - hot steamed rice.

Figs Curry Recipe

A simple but unique dish, prepared with figs fruit. This is a very popular recipe within the regions of Himachal.

Serves – 3 persons
Time – 30 minutes

Ingredients

250 gm figs (cut in half)
½ tsp cumin powder
1 tsp turmeric powder
3 cloves
1 small bay leaf
1 tsp coriander powder
1 inch finely chopped ginger piece
½ tsp red chilli powder
½ tsp black pepper powder
3 finely chopped green chilli
5 finely chopped garlic
1 big finely chopped onion
Mustard oil
Salt to taste

Preparation

1.   Take a pan and heat mustard oil. Next add bay leaves, cloves, onion, ginger and garlic, fry until the onion turns golden brown in color.

2.   Now add figs, cumin seeds powder, salt, red chilli powder, turmeric powder, coriander powder, black pepper powder and mix them well.
3.   Add water and pressure cook for 1 whistle. Serve hot.

Best Served with - rice or any kind of chapattis.

Chana Masala (Garbanzo Bean Curry)

Chana dal is one of the more popular dishes found at Indian restaurants and originates from the state of Punjab. Though this dish makes appearance only on special occasions in a regular Indian household. With a bit of preparation, this dish comes together in no time and can be prepared ahead of time and stored for weekday meals. Traditionally this dish is made from dried chickpeas, 2 can of 15 ounce chickpea can be substituted for 1 ½ cup dried chickpeas used in this recipe.

Serves - 4 persons
Time – 55 minutes

Ingredients

1 ½ cup dried chickpeas

1 tsp baking soda

2 inch piece of fresh ginger, grated or finely chopped

3 cloves garlic, roughly chopped

3 Tbsp olive oil

2 medium onions, sliced

1 28-ounce can of plum tomatoes

1 Tbsp tomato paste

1 tsp ground cumin

1 tsp garam masala

½ tsp turmeric powder

1 ½ tsp salt, or to taste

For garnish:

Lemon wedges

Chopped cilantro

Sliced red onions

1. Night before, rinse and soak the dried beans in a large pot. Add baking soda and cover with water and soak for 8 to 10 hours or overnight.
2. The day of – Rinse and drain the beans. In a large soup pot, cover the beans with cold water and bring to boil for 45-50 minutes, until soft, discard any scum.
3. Make a paste of ginger, garlic and salt.
4. Heat a wide-bottomed large frying pan with oil. When it's hot, add the onions and cook for 12 to 15 minutes until golden brown. When the onions are caramelized add the ginger, garlic paste and stir to mix. Add the tomatoes to the mixture crushing them with your hand before they hit the pan. Add the tomato paste, stir well and cook for 10 minutes.

5. Add the spices – garam masala, ground cumin, turmeric and more salt if necessary. Cook for a few minutes. Add the cooked chickpeas to the mixture. Stir to mix and check for consistency. Add ¼ cup of water if necessary. Continue to cook for 10 minutes.
6. Remove from the heat. Garnish with cilantro.

Best served with - naan, steamed rice

Griddle Chicken Recipe

A fantastic sizzling dish from the state of Himachal containing a combination of tempering red chillies and coriander leaves, perfect for a wintery dinner party!

Serves - 4 persons
Time – 85 minutes

Ingredients
Chicken (7 pieces)

For Marinade
1 cup hung curd
2 tbsp cream
1 tsp ginger-garlic paste
3 tsp grounded spice

For grounded spices
2 cinnamon sticks
12 black peppercorns
½ tsp cumin seeds
7 cardamom green
2 cardamom brown
3 cloves
2 bay leaves

For main preparation
1 tbsp oil
1 tsp salt
½ tsp lemon juice

For tempering

1 tbsp oil
2 tbsp chopped coriander leaves
3 dried red chillies
4 whole red chilli
½ tsp turmeric powder

Preparation

1.   Grind all grounded spices to fine powder.
2.   Add the chicken pieces to a bowl, followed by turmeric powder, ginger-garlic paste, salt, cream, hung curd and grounded spices then mix all together, set aside to marinate for an hour.
3.   In a pan add oil, then all the marinated chicken pieces. Cook well until the meat becomes tender and brown in texture.
4.   Using another pan, add oil followed by dried red chillies and coriander leaves, Sauté for a minute.
5.   Finally, sprinkle some grounded spice and lemon juice onto the top of the chicken and pour the prepared seasoning over it. Serve hot.

Best served with - chapattis or steamed rice.

Chicken Coconut Cashew Sauce

From the state of Uttar Pradesh, this recipe is a clear favorite amongst many, due to the chicken which is stuffed with delicious cheese and cashew.

Serves – 2 persons
Time – 50 minutes

Ingredients

4 pieces of chicken breast
1 ½ tsp ginger paste
½ tsp yellow chilli powder
½ tsp cumin seeds
2 tsp garlic paste
Salt to taste

For the stuffing

½ cup of concentrated milk
½ cup of grated cheese
½ cup of finely chopped onions
Handful of peeled pomegranate seeds
2 tbsp chopped coriander leaves
1 tbsp chopped chillies
½ tsp ginger
½ juiced lemon
Salt to taste

For the chicken

1 tbsp clarified butter
Few black cardamoms
4-5 green cardamoms
Cinnamon
1 piece small mace
Handful of black pepper

For the sauce

½ cup of cashew nuts
½ cup of desiccated coconut powder
½ tsp black cardamom powder
1 tbsp clarified butter
1 cup of finely chopped onions
2 tsp garlic paste
1 tsp ginger paste
½ cup of whipped yogurt
Salt to taste
½ tsp fennel powder
½ tsp green cardamom powder
1 tsp yellow chilli powder
A pinch of mace powder
A pinch of nutmeg powder

Preparation

1. Remove all fat from the chicken breast pieces, then flatten the breast from inside only using the blunt end of a knife.
2. Next mix all spices to prepare the marinade for the chicken, then coat the chicken completely with the marinade spice. Leave to marinate for 15 minutes.
3. In a bowl, mix well all the stuffing ingredients. Next lay the chicken pieces flat and stuff with the mixture. Ensure the mixture remains at one end of the chicken then roll the chicken breast.

For the chicken

4. Now in a pan heat some clarified butter, followed by some black cardamom, green cardamom and all the spices. Once the spices begin to splutter, add some water approx. 2 cups.

5. Gently introduce the folded side of the chicken to the liquid so that it doesn't open up. Cover with foil paper and leave to cook for 2-3 minutes. In the mean-time the sauce can be prepared.

For the sauce

1. Fry roast the coconut and cashew nuts in a pan, then add to a blender with some water to make a fine paste.

2. Heat some clarified butter in a pan, add onions and leave to fry until a golden- brown texture is achieved, then add ginger-garlic paste and leave to brown.

3. Now add yogurt and salt. Once the yogurt starts to cook and the fat separates completely, add the coconut and cashew paste. Whilst this takes place it is time to add all the other spices and mix well.

4. Now add about ½ cup of water to maintain consistency and add 2 tbsp of chicken juice to the sauce.

5. When chicken is cooked well, place on a plate and when the sauce reaches a good thickness remove from flame. Pour over chicken and serve.

Best served with - steamed rice or chapattis.

Watermelon Rind Curry

This curry is from the dry regions of Rajasthan where watermelon is a very essential product. In this recipe the rind is used to achieve a healthy dish.

Serves – 4 persons
Time – 30 minutes

Ingredients

4 cups watermelon rind, tough green skin removed and cut into ½ inch pieces
2 tbsp clarified butter
1 inch minced ginger
½ green chilli (minced & seeds removed)
5 minced cloves of garlic
¼ tsp turmeric powder
½ tsp cumin seeds
½ tsp dried mango powder
1 tsp coriander powder
1 tsp pepper
¼ tsp red chilli powder
¼ tsp grounded spices
Salt to taste

Preparation

1. In a pan heat some clarified butter followed by cumin seeds, ginger, garlic, green chillies and roast gently.
2. Now add the watermelon rind and stir fry it for a minute. Add red chilli powder, pepper, turmeric, fry mango powder and salt. Cover with lid, leave to cook for 15 minutes, continue to stir periodically.

3.   Once the rind gets tenderized and dry, add grounded spices to it and mix it well. Serve hot.

Best served with - chapattis.

Conclusion

I hope these recipes have helped you gain an appreciation of the fusion of tastes that Northern Indian dishes provide. From the chilled mountains to dry desert and the land of gods, every dish is unique in its own special way. Northern Indian cuisine has so much to offer and if you are a foodie, I hope the recipes have encouraged you to one day visit the region, where you will find a vast array of food habits and cooking styles.

If you're craving even more Indian recipes and would like a great selection of curries for any dietary preference, then grab a copy of my popular curry cookbook, containing 50 recipes;

The Greatest Indian Curries Ever Created!

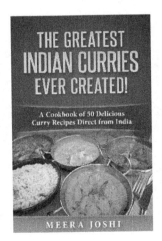

Just a reminder...don't forget to visit **www.ffdrecipes.com** for your FREE bonus recipe ebooks and to get exclusive access to our VIP World Recipes Club, which provides FREE book offers, discounts and recipe ideas!

Thank you.

Cooking Measurements & Conversions

Oven Temperature Conversions

Use the below table as a guide to establishing the correct temperatures when cooking, however please be aware that oven types and models and location of your kitchen can have an influence on temperature also.

°F	°C	Gas Mark	Explanation
275°F	140°C	1	cool
300°F	150°C	2	
325°F	170°C	3	very moderate
350°F	180°C	4	moderate
375°F	190°C	5	
400°F	200°C	6	moderately hot
425°F	220°C	7	hot
450°F	230°C	8	
475°F	240°C	9	very hot

US to Metric Corresponding Measures

Metric	Imperial
3 teaspoons	1 tablespoon
1 tablespoon	1/16 cup
2 tablespoons	1/8 cup
2 tablespoons + 2 teaspoons	1/6 cup
4 tablespoons	1/4 cup
5 tablespoons + 1 teaspoon	1/3 cup
6 tablespoons	3/8 cup
8 tablespoons	½ cup
10 tablespoons + 2 teaspoons	2/3 cup
12 tablespoons	3/4 cup
16 tablespoons	1 cup
48 teaspoons	1 cup

8 fluid ounces (fl oz)	1 cup
1 pint	2 cups
1 quart	2 pints
1 quart	4 cups
1 gallon (gal)	4 quarts
1 cubic centimeter (cc)	1 milliliter (ml)
2.54 centimeters (cm)	1 inch (in)
1 pound (lb)	16 ounces (oz)

Liquid to Volume

Metric	Imperial
15ml	1 tbsp
55 ml	2 fl oz
75 ml	3 fl oz
150 ml	5 fl oz (¼ pint)
275 ml	10 fl oz (½ pint)
570 ml	1 pint
725 ml	1 ¼ pints
1 litre	1 ¾ pints
1.2 litres	2 pints
1.5 litres	2½ pints
2.25 litres	4 pints

Weight Conversion

Metric	Imperial
10 g	½ oz
20 g	¾ oz
25 g	1 oz
40 g	1½ oz
50 g	2 oz
60 g	2½ oz
75 g	3 oz
110 g	4 oz
125 g	4½ oz
150 g	5 oz
175 g	6 oz
200 g	7 oz
225 g	8 oz
250 g	9 oz
275 g	10 oz

350 g	12 oz
450 g	1 lb
700 g	1 lb 8 oz
900 g	2 lb
1.35 kg	3 lb

G

Cooking Abbreviations

Abbreviation	Description
tsp	teaspoon
Tbsp	tablespoon
c	cup
pt	pint
qt	quart
gal	gallon
wt	weight
oz	ounce
lb	pound
g	gram
kg	kilogram
vol	volume
ml	milliliter
fl oz	fluid ounce

Made in the USA
Monee, IL
23 November 2020